MW01225398

Mandala Me

Love

Coloring Book

PK Burian

PK Burian © 2016 Blue Light Publishing

Cover Illustrated by KP Azeltine

ISBN 13: 978-1523755189

ISBN 10: 1523755180

About The Author

 PK Burian loved coloring as a child. She colored and loved to draw throughout her teens and college years. As a parent, she taught her daughters coloring and crafts. She couldn't be happier that adults are returning to an activity that once brought her and them such joy.

A writer of romance, young adult paranormal, middle-grade mystery, and picture books, she is happy to bring coloring books to adults, teens, and children.

You can find PK Burian at pkburian.com and pkburiancoloringbooks.com

Go To: **pkburian.com** or

pkburiancoloringbooks.com

For more Mandala Me Coloring Books look for:

Mandala Me Beautiful
Mandala Me Animals
Mandala Me Paisley
Mandala Me Paisley Pretty
Mandala Me Love
Mandala Me Hearts

And for kids:

Animals of the Forest
Bears, Bears, Bears Coloring Book
Bears, Bears, Bears Activity Book
Birds of a Feather
Butterflies Everywhere
Happy Farm Animals
My Favorite Pet
More coming soon!

35361707R00031

Made in the USA
Middletown, DE
29 September 2016